delicious diabetic recipes

Decadent Chocolate

Table of Contents

Chocolate Chip Angel Food Cake Kabobs with Strawberry Sauce

         1 package (16 ounces) angel food cake mix
       1/3 cup mini chocolate chips
        24 small fresh strawberries
            Strawberry Sauce (recipe follows)

1. Preheat oven to 350°F. Prepare cake mix according to package directions; stir chocolate chips into batter. Gently spoon batter into 3 (8¼×4¼-inch) loaf pans.

2. Bake 28 minutes or until golden brown. Cool completely in pans on wire racks. Remove from pans; wrap and freeze 2 cakes for another use. Cut third cake into 6 slices; gently tear or cut each slice into 4 pieces.

3. Alternate 3 cake pieces and 3 strawberries on each of 8 wooden skewers. Prepare and serve with Strawberry Sauce.   *Makes 8 servings*

Strawberry Sauce

        1 cup sliced fresh strawberries
        1 tablespoon sugar
        1 teaspoon lemon juice
       ¼ cup water
        1 teaspoon cornstarch

Combine strawberries, sugar and lemon juice in small saucepan. Whisk water and cornstarch in small bowl until smooth and well blended; stir into strawberry mixture. Bring to a boil over high heat. Reduce heat to low; simmer 1 minute or until thickened, stirring constantly. Purée mixture using hand-held immersion blender or transfer mixture to food processor or blender; process until smooth.   *Makes about 1 cup*

Serving Size: 1 skewer with about 2 tablespoons sauce
Calories 130, **Total Fat** 2g, **Saturated Fat** 1g,
Protein 2g, **Carbohydrate** 27g, **Cholesterol** 0mg,
Dietary Fiber 2g, **Sodium** 140mg

Dietary Exchanges: 2 Starch

Pumpkin Softies with Chocolate Drizzle

- 1¼ cups all-purpose flour
- 1 teaspoon baking powder
- ½ teaspoon baking soda
- ½ teaspoon ground cinnamon
- ½ teaspoon ground nutmeg
- ¼ teaspoon salt
- ¾ cup packed brown sugar
- ¼ cup (½ stick) butter, softened
- ½ cup canned solid-pack pumpkin
- 1 egg
- ½ teaspoon vanilla
- ⅓ cup semisweet chocolate chips

1. Preheat oven to 350°F. Line cookie sheets with parchment paper.

2. Combine flour, baking powder, baking soda, cinnamon, nutmeg and salt in medium bowl; mix well. Beat brown sugar and butter in large bowl with electric mixer at medium speed until well blended. Add pumpkin, egg and vanilla; beat until smooth and well blended. Gradually add flour mixture, beating well after each addition. (Dough will be consistency of thick cake batter). Drop dough by rounded tablespoonfuls 2 inches apart onto prepared cookie sheets.

3. Bake 13 to 15 minutes or until edges are firm to touch. Cool on cookie sheets 2 minutes. Remove to wire racks; cool completely.

4. Place chocolate chips in small resealable food storage bag; seal bag. Microwave on HIGH at 30-second intervals until chocolate is melted. Knead bag until smooth. Cut off tiny corner of bag; drizzle chocolate over cookies. Let stand until set. *Makes 2 dozen cookies*

Serving Size: 1 cookie
Calories 84, **Total Fat** 3g, **Saturated Fat** 2g,
Protein 1g, **Carbohydrate** 14g, **Cholesterol** 13mg,
Dietary Fiber 0g, **Sodium** 93mg

Dietary Exchanges: 1 Starch, ½ Fat

Frozen Chocolate-Covered Bananas

 2 medium ripe bananas

 4 pop sticks

 ½ cup granola cereal without raisins

 1 bottle (7¼ ounces) quick-hardening chocolate shell dessert topping

1. Line baking sheet with waxed paper.

2. Peel bananas; cut each in half crosswise. Insert stick about 1½ inches into center of cut end of each banana. Place on prepared baking sheet. Freeze 2 hours or until firm.

3. Place granola in large resealable food storage bag; crush slightly using rolling pin or meat mallet. Transfer granola to shallow dish. Pour chocolate shell topping in separate shallow dish.

4. Place one frozen banana in topping; turn and spread evenly over banana with spatula. Immediately place banana in dish with granola, turning to coat evenly. Return to baking sheet. Repeat with remaining bananas.

5. Freeze 2 hours or until firm. Let stand 5 minutes before serving.

Makes 4 servings

tip For a fun twist on these treats, roll in sprinkles, coconut, chopped peanuts or any other desired toppings.

Serving Size: ½ banana
Calories 191, **Total Fat** 4g, **Saturated Fat** 2g,
Protein 3g, **Carbohydrate** 38g, **Cholesterol** 3mg,
Dietary Fiber 3g, **Sodium** 132mg

Dietary Exchanges: 1½ Starch, ½ Fat, 1 Fruit

Chocolate-Coffee Napoleons

- ¼ cup hot water
- 1 tablespoon instant coffee granules
- 1 package (4-serving size) chocolate fat-free sugar-free instant pudding and pie filling mix
- 1¾ cups plus 1 teaspoon whole milk, divided
- 1 sheet frozen puff pastry, thawed
- 3 tablespoons powdered sugar
- 2 tablespoons bittersweet or semisweet chocolate chips

1. Combine water and coffee granules in small cup; stir until coffee granules are completely dissolved. Cool completely.

2. Prepare pudding mix according to package directions using 1¾ cups milk and coffee. Cover and refrigerate until ready to use.

3. Preheat oven to 400°F. Line baking sheet with parchment paper. Unfold pastry sheet; cut into 3 strips along folds. Cut each strip crosswise into thirds, forming 9 squares. Place on prepared baking sheet. Bake 12 to 15 minutes or until puffed and golden brown. Remove to wire rack; cool completely.

4. Whisk powdered sugar and remaining 1 teaspoon milk in small bowl until smooth. Cut each pastry square in half crosswise using serrated knife to form 18 pieces total. Spread icing over tops of 6 pastry pieces.

5. Place chocolate chips in small resealable food storage bag; seal bag. Microwave on HIGH at 30-second intervals until chocolate is melted. Knead bag until smooth. Cut off tiny corner of bag; drizzle chocolate over iced pastry pieces. Let stand until set.

6. Spoon about 2 tablespoons pudding mixture over each of 6 pastry pieces; layer with remaining 6 pastry pieces and pudding mixture. Top with iced pastry pieces. Refrigerate until ready to serve. *Makes 6 napoleons*

Serving Size: 1 napoleon
Calories 139, **Total Fat** 7g, **Saturated Fat** 3g,
Protein 4g, **Carbohydrate** 18g, **Cholesterol** 7mg,
Dietary Fiber 1g, **Sodium** 124 mg

Dietary Exchanges: 1 Starch, 1½ Fat

Oat, Chocolate and Hazelnut Biscotti

1½ cups whole wheat flour

1 cup all-purpose flour

1 cup old-fashioned oats

2 teaspoons baking powder

½ teaspoon salt

½ teaspoon ground cinnamon

1½ cups sugar

½ cup (1 stick) unsalted butter, softened

3 eggs

1 teaspoon vanilla

2 cups toasted hazelnuts*

¾ cup semisweet chocolate chunks

To toast hazelnuts, spread in single layer on ungreased baking sheet. Bake in preheated 350°F oven 8 to 10 minutes or until golden brown, stirring occasionally. Cool before using.

1. Preheat oven to 325°F. Line cookie sheet with parchment paper.

2. Combine flours, oats, baking powder, salt and cinnamon in large bowl; mix well. Beat sugar and butter in large bowl with electric mixer at high speed until light and fluffy. Beat in eggs and vanilla. Gradually beat in flour mixture at low speed until well blended. Fold in hazelnuts and chocolate chips.

3. Divide dough into 2 pieces. Shape each piece into 10×3-inch log. Place on prepared cookie sheet.

4. Bake 30 minutes. Cool completely on baking sheet. *Reduce oven temperature to 300°F.* Transfer logs to cutting board; cut diagonally into ½-inch slices using serrated knife. Arrange slices, cut sides up, on cookie sheet. Bake 10 to 15 minutes or until golden brown. Turn slices over; bake 5 to 10 minutes or until golden brown. Remove to wire racks; cool completely.

Makes 4 dozen biscotti

Serving Size: 1 biscotti
Calories 120, **Total Fat** 6g, **Saturated Fat** 2g,
Protein 2g, **Carbohydrate** 15g, **Cholesterol** 18mg,
Dietary Fiber 1g, **Sodium** 50mg

Dietary Exchanges: 1 Starch, 1 Fat

Chocolate Cookie Parfaits

1 package (4-serving size) chocolate fat-free sugar-free instant pudding and pie filling mix

2 cups fat-free (skim) milk

8 tablespoons thawed reduced-fat whipped topping

4 sugar-free chocolate sandwich cookies, finely crushed

4 teaspoons multi-colored sprinkles

1. Prepare pudding according to package directions using 2 cups milk.

2. Spoon half of pudding in 4 dessert dishes. Top each with 1 tablespoon whipped topping. Sprinkle evenly with half of crushed cookies. Layer remaining pudding over top of cookies. Top with remaining whipped topping, cookies and sprinkles. *Makes 4 servings*

Serving Size: 1 parfait
Calories 158, **Total Fat** 6g, **Saturated Fat** 2g,
Protein 6g, **Carbohydrate** 24g, **Cholesterol** 2mg,
Dietary Fiber 0g, **Sodium** 387mg

Dietary Exchanges: 1 Starch, 1 Fat, ½ Milk

Trail Mix Truffles

⅓ cup dried apples

¼ cup dried apricots

¼ cup apple butter

2 tablespoons golden raisins

1 tablespoon reduced-fat creamy or chunky peanut butter

½ cup reduced-fat granola

¼ cup graham cracker crumbs, divided

¼ cup mini chocolate chips

1 tablespoon water

1. Combine apples, apricots, apple butter, raisins and peanut butter in food processor or blender; process until smooth. Stir in granola, 1 tablespoon graham cracker crumbs, chocolate chips and water. Shape mixture into 16 balls.

2. Place remaining graham cracker crumbs in shallow dish; roll balls in crumbs. Cover and refrigerate until ready to serve. *Makes 16 truffles*

Serving Size: 2 truffles
Calories 121, **Total Fat** 4g, **Saturated Fat** 1g,
Protein 3g, **Carbohydrate** 20g, **Cholesterol** 0mg,
Dietary Fiber 2g, **Sodium** 14mg

Dietary Exchanges: 1 Starch, ½ Fat, ½ Fruit

Chocolate Chip, Banana and Marshmallow Triangles

1 package (6½ ounces) chocolate chip muffin mix

½ cup water

1 medium banana, sliced

½ cup mini marshmallows

⅓ cup coarsely chopped pecans, toasted*

*To toast pecans, spread in single layer on ungreased baking sheet. Bake in preheated 350°F oven 8 to 10 minutes or until fragrant, stirring occasionally. Cool before using.

1. Preheat oven to 375°F. Spray 8-inch square baking pan with nonstick cooking spray.

2. Stir muffin mix and water in medium bowl just until blended. Spoon into prepared pan. Layer banana slices over batter; sprinkle with marshmallows and pecans.

3. Bake 30 minutes or until marshmallows begin to brown. Cool completely on wire rack. Cut into 4 squares; cut each square in half diagonally to create 8 triangles. *Makes 8 servings*

Serving Size: 1 triangle
Calories 151, **Total Fat** 6g, **Saturated Fat** 1g,
Protein 2g, **Carbohydrate** 24g, **Cholesterol** 1mg,
Dietary Fiber 1g, **Sodium** 106mg

Dietary Exchanges: 1½ Starch, 1 Fat

Chocolate-Frosted Peanut Butter Cupcakes

1¾	cups all-purpose flour
1½	teaspoons baking powder
¼	teaspoon salt
⅓	cup (⅔ stick) butter, softened
⅓	cup reduced-fat creamy or chunky peanut butter
½	cup granulated sugar
¼	cup packed brown sugar
2	eggs
1	teaspoon vanilla
1¼	cups milk
	Peanut Butter Chocolate Frosting (recipe follows)

1. Preheat oven to 350°F. Line 18 standard (2½-inch) muffin cups with paper or foil baking cups.

2. Combine flour, baking powder and salt in medium bowl; mix well. Beat butter and peanut butter in large bowl with electric mixer at medium speed until smooth. Add granulated sugar and brown sugar; beat until well blended. Add eggs and vanilla; beat until well blended. Alternately add flour mixture and milk, beating well after each addition. Spoon evenly into prepared muffin cups.

3. Bake 25 minutes or until toothpick inserted into centers comes out clean. Cool in pans 10 minutes. Remove to wire racks; cool completely.

4. Prepare Peanut Butter Chocolate Frosting. Frost cupcakes.

Makes 18 cupcakes

Peanut Butter Chocolate Frosting

4	cups powdered sugar
⅓	cup unsweetened cocoa powder
4 to 6	tablespoons milk, divided
3	tablespoons creamy peanut butter

Beat powdered sugar, cocoa, 4 tablespoons milk and peanut butter in large bowl with electric mixer at low speed until smooth. Beat in additional milk, 1 tablespoon at a time, until desired consistency is reached.

Makes about 2½ cups

Serving Size: 1 cupcake
Calories 201, **Total Fat** 7g, **Saturated Fat** 2g,
Protein 4g, **Carbohydrate** 32g, **Cholesterol** 18mg,
Dietary Fiber 1g, **Sodium** 134mg

Dietary Exchanges: 2 Starch, 1 Fat

Chocolate Chip Frozen Yogurt

   1 cup plain nonfat yogurt

   ½ cup fat-free half-and-half

   2 tablespoons sugar

   ¼ teaspoon vanilla

   ¼ cup mini semisweet chocolate chips

1. Stir yogurt, half-and-half, sugar and vanilla in medium bowl until well blended.

2. Freeze yogurt mixture in ice cream maker according to manufacturer's directions until soft. Add chocolate chips; freeze until firm.

Makes 6 servings

Serving Size: ⅓ cup
Calories 87, **Total Fat** 2g, **Saturated Fat** 1g,
Protein 3g, **Carbohydrate** 14g, **Cholesterol** 4mg,
Dietary Fiber 1g, **Sodium** 52mg

Dietary Exchanges: 1 Starch, ½ Fat

Flourless Chocolate Cake

- 3 squares (1 ounce each) semisweet chocolate, chopped
- 3 tablespoons margarine
- 1 tablespoon instant coffee granules
- 2 tablespoons hot water
- 4 eggs, separated
- 2 egg whites
- ⅔ cup sugar, divided
- 3 tablespoons unsweetened cocoa powder
- 1 teaspoon vanilla
- ½ teaspoon salt
- Whipped topping (optional)
- Fresh raspberries (optional)
- Fresh mint leaves (optional)

1. Preheat oven to 300°F. Spray 9-inch springform pan with nonstick cooking spray; line bottom of pan with parchment paper.

2. Melt chocolate and margarine in small heavy saucepan over low heat, stirring frequently; cool completely. Combine water and coffee granules in small cup; stir until coffee granules are completely dissolved. Cool completely.

3. Place 6 egg whites in large bowl; set aside. Beat egg yolks in medium bowl with electric mixer at high speed 5 minutes or until pale yellow in color. Add ⅓ cup sugar; beat 4 minutes or until mixture falls in ribbons from beaters. Slowly beat in melted chocolate mixture and espresso mixture at low speed just until blended. Beat in cocoa and vanilla just until blended.

4. Add salt to egg whites; beat at high speed 2 minutes or until soft peaks form. Beat in remaining ⅓ cup sugar until stiff peaks form. Stir large spoonful of egg whites into chocolate mixture. Fold chocolate mixture into egg whites until almost blended. Spoon batter into prepared pan.

5. Bake 1 hour or until cake begins to pull away from side of pan. Cool on wire rack 10 minutes; run thin spatula around edge of cake. Carefully remove side of pan. Cool completely. Invert cake; remove bottom of pan and paper from cake. Cover and refrigerate at least 4 hours. Serve chilled with whipped topping, raspberries and mint, if desired. *Makes 10 servings*

Serving Size: 1 slice
Calories 190, **Total Fat** 8g, **Saturated Fat** 3g,
Protein 4g, **Carbohydrate** 26g, **Cholesterol** 85mg,
Dietary Fiber 1g, **Sodium** 240mg

Dietary Exchanges: 1½ Starch, 1 Fat

Chocolate Chip-Cherry Oatmeal Cookies

⅔ cup sugar

⅓ cup canola oil

¼ cup cholesterol-free egg substitute

1 teaspoon vanilla

¾ cup all-purpose flour

½ teaspoon baking soda

½ teaspoon ground cinnamon

⅛ teaspoon salt

1½ cups quick oats

½ cup dried cherries, raisins or cranberries

¼ cup mini semisweet chocolate chips

1. Preheat oven to 325°F. Spray cookie sheets with nonstick cooking spray.

2. Beat sugar, oil, egg substitute and vanilla in large bowl with electric mixer at medium speed until well blended. Add flour, baking soda, cinnamon and salt; beat until well blended. Stir in oats, dried cherries and chocolate chips. Drop dough by slightly rounded teaspoonfuls about 2 inches apart onto prepared cookie sheets.

3. Bake 7 minutes (cookies will not brown). Cool on cookie sheets 2 minutes. Remove to wire racks; cool completely.   *Makes 4 dozen cookies*

Serving Size: 2 cookies
Calories 103, **Total Fat** 4g, **Saturated Fat** 1g,
Protein 1g, **Carbohydrate** 16g, **Cholesterol** 0mg,
Dietary Fiber 1g, **Sodium** 45mg

Dietary Exchanges: 1 Starch, 1 Fat

Chocolate Chip Muffins

1¾ cups all-purpose flour

⅓ cup packed brown sugar

2 tablespoons unsweetened cocoa powder

2½ teaspoons baking powder

1½ teaspoons ground cinnamon

¼ teaspoon salt

1 cup fat-free (skim) milk

1 egg, lightly beaten

¼ cup unsweetened applesauce

2 tablespoons butter, melted

1 teaspoon vanilla

⅔ cup mini semisweet chocolate chips

1. Preheat oven to 400°F. Spray 12 standard (2½-inch) muffin cups with nonstick cooking spray or line with foil baking cups.

2. Combine flour, brown sugar, cocoa, baking powder, cinnamon and salt in medium bowl. Whisk milk, egg, applesauce, butter and vanilla in small bowl until blended. Stir into flour mixture just until blended. Fold in chocolate chips. Spoon evenly into prepared muffin cups.

3. Bake 13 to 15 minutes or until toothpick inserted into centers comes out clean. Cool in pan 5 minutes. Remove to wire rack; cool completely.

Makes 12 muffins

Serving Size: 1 muffin
Calories 172, **Total Fat** 6g, **Saturated Fat** 3g,
Protein 4g, **Carbohydrate** 29g, **Cholesterol** 23mg,
Dietary Fiber 2g, **Sodium** 182mg

Dietary Exchanges: 1½ Starch, 1 Fat

Chocolate Peanut Butter Fondue

⅓ cup sugar

⅓ cup unsweetened cocoa powder

⅓ cup low-fat (1%) milk

3 tablespoons light corn syrup

2 tablespoons reduced-fat peanut butter

½ teaspoon vanilla

Assorted fresh fruit, pretzel rods and/or pound cake cubes

1. Combine sugar, cocoa, milk, corn syrup and peanut butter in medium saucepan. Cook over medium heat until heated through, stirring constantly. Remove from heat; stir in vanilla.

2. Pour into medium bowl. Serve warm or at room temperature with fruit, pretzels and/or pound cake cubes for dipping. *Makes 8 servings*

Calories 242, **Total Fat** 4g, **Saturated Fat** 1g, **Protein** 4g, **Carbohydrate** 50g, **Cholesterol** 14mg, **Dietary Fiber** 2g, **Sodium** 30mg

Dietary Exchanges: 2 Starch, 1 Fat, 2 Fruit